CW00664878

GOD'S MAGIC

An Aspect of Spiritualism

by

AIR CHIEF MARSHAL
LORD DOWDING

By the same Author
TWELVE LEGIONS OF ANGELS
MANY MANSIONS
LYCHGATE
THE DARK STAR

www.whitecrowbooks.com

God's Magic

Original copyright © 1960 by Air Chief Marshal Lord Dowding
This Copyright © 2015 by David Whiting. All rights reserved.

Published and printed in the United States of America and the United Kingdom
by White Crow Books; an imprint of White Crow Productions Ltd.

No part of this book may be reproduced, copied or used in any form
or manner whatsoever without written permission, except in the
case of brief quotations in reviews and critical articles.

For information, contact White Crow Books
at 3 Hova Villas, Hove, BN3 3 DH United Kingdom,
or e-mail to info@whitecrowbooks.com.

Cover Designed by Butterflyeffect
Interior design by Velin@Perseus-Design.com

Paperback ISBN 978-1-910121-67-2
eBook   ISBN 978-1-910121-68-9

Non Fiction / Body, Mind & Spirit / Spiritualism / Death & Dying

www.whitecrowbooks.com

Disclaimer: White Crow Productions Ltd. and its directors, employees, distributors,
retailers, wholesalers and assignees disclaim any liability or responsibility for
the author's statements, words, ideas, criticisms or observations. White Crow
Productions Ltd. assumes no responsibility for errors, inaccuracies, or omissions.

GOD'S MAGIC

CONTENTS

INTRODUCTION

———————➤●◄———————

T his book is mainly about what is generally known as Spiritualism, though personally I am not much in love with the word.

It is one of a series which is being written on the same subject and it is strictly limited in length.

I shall try, therefore, to avoid covering again that ground which I know will be adequately covered by the other contributors to the series, and to concentrate on those aspects of the subject which specially appeal to me and of which I have had some personal experience.

I shall not devote much of my limited space to an attempt to prove human survival after death, and the possibility of communicating with those who have died. Most people, when they approach this subject, seem to demand that one single instance shall be adduced, so much beyond criticism, so water tight in all its joints, that scepticism is unwillingly swept away in an irresistible torrent of certitude.

Well, in my experience, that is not the way in which conviction comes. Not that there is any difficulty in finding such instances, but the ignorant sceptic is so mistrustful of his own judgment, so afraid of being thought unduly credulous by his friends, that he will devise all sorts of explanations for the phenomena—some of them much more complicated and improbable than the simple truth which is their alternative. If all else fails he will just say that the facts are not as reported.

It is a strange thing, indeed, that the existence of phenomena which have been since the first days of man's habitation of this earth should still be the subject of any difference of opinion among intelligent and educated persons; it is strange that knowledge, once it has become the property of humanity, can pass out of circulation into oblivion.

How astonished would have been those astronomers who laid out Stonehenge, or who oriented the Pyramids, if they had been told that ten thousand years after they were dead the official scientists of the world's most powerful nations would not only believe that the sun and the stars revolved round the earth daily, but would persecute anyone who advanced a contrary hypothesis.

But so it has been. For the purposes of evolution, it has been necessary that man should descend into the very depths of Materialism. This he has done with alacrity, and we see the results when we look around us at the world today. But man has passed the lowest point, and his enlightenment to the things of the Spirit has already begun.

I am optimist enough to believe that in this new age now beginning—this Aquarian Age—the flame of knowledge and enlightenment will spread like wildfire. It will be a poor lookout for the world if I am wrong, for mankind has been headed for destruction and has not missed that goal by much; but I don't think I am wrong.

Not, mind you, that a mere belief in human survival after death and in the possibility of communicating with those survivors, is going to take us very far by itself; it is quite possible to accept the elementary facts of Spiritualism and yet remain substantially a materialist in one's personal life. I regard this acceptance rather as a door opening onto new vistas and a fresh outlook on life.

It is not much use preaching at humanity—telling them that they must deny themselves earthly pleasures and satisfactions, mortify the flesh, despise wealth and power, and suffer injuries with patience and forgiveness, unless the preacher is prepared to enter into an intelligent discussion as to where all this altruism and self-sacrifice is going to lead.

True there is always a certain section of the population which is prepared to be convinced by abstract arguments, to be righteous for righteousness sake, to follow uncritically the light of religion kindled in childhood; but nowadays such people are in a small minority. The bulk of the population of Protestant countries are neither attracted by the nebulous promises of an orthodox heaven nor alarmed by the threat of an orthodox hell. They are not basically irreligious; on occasions of great national danger or triumph they will flock to their churches to join in supplication or thanksgiving as the occasion demands; the bulk of them are fundamentally decent and charitable and law abiding, but organised religion stands for nothing in their lives.

The Roman Church exercises a stricter discipline over its adherents, but the outcome expressed in terms of morality does not seem to be greatly superior.

It seems to me that if the average human being is to be persuaded to abandon his instinctive reactions to the stimuli of life and to follow the road of consideration for others, which alone can lead to escape from the present predicament of humanity, the question of the details of the future life (so far as they can be known) and the results in the next life of causes initiated here on earth, must be faced and investigated with all diligence and honesty of mind.

Communication with those who have passed the boundary of death, and have actually experienced the conditions of which they speak, is quite obviously a means of information which we shall be very foolish to ignore, provided we can satisfy ourselves that such communication is possible.

As I say, the other contributors to this series will supply the material on which a judgment may be formed. If their testimony is considered invalid, there are volumes and libraries full of further evidence. And it is important to remember that you have only to be convinced of the truth and accuracy of one case, to be convinced that true communication with the other side is possible.

But, having convinced yourself of this, do not fly to the other extreme and believe that every message coming from the other side must necessarily be true. I wish that this were so, but it is unfortunately far from being the case.

All that I, or anyone else, can fairly claim is that discarnate communication is one of the most valuable and prolific methods by which humanity may attain to some approximation to knowledge of conditions on the other side of physical death, and that those who refuse to avail themselves of this potential source of information are deliberately ignoring something of great importance to themselves.

Conviction, as I have said, does not normally come through one single specific instance of spirit communication (though this is often the case where personal contact is made with a close friend or relation). It comes normally by an almost unnoticed accretion of evidence which piles up if the subject is continuously studied. It is a sort of subconscious reckoning of mathematical odds, until the odds in favour of at least one of the events being true become quite overwhelming. I don't know if I can be considered to be a typical student of these matters, but personally I soon found my interest shifting to the contents of communications and away from the circumstances of their receipt. I stopped saying to myself: "Is the medium cheating?" because I found that in my own personal experience mediums did not cheat. On the other hand they were sometimes wrong, and the important thing was to know whether the message was true or false; it was only of secondary importance to trace the cause when something had gone wrong.

I have read so many books on Spiritualism which ignore this very important aspect. One would think from reading them that with an honest medium nothing ever went wrong.

This leaves it to be inferred by ignorant people that, if a medium is wrong, he or she is dishonest; this is not at all true, but it is the cause of a very widespread impression among the uninstructed public that fraud is rife.

I have neither the space nor the wish to elaborate this aspect of Spiritualism just now, but remember that mediumship is only a telephone line between the worlds and that it is not always possible to determine who has pressed Button A at the other end. Add to this the consideration that people do not, by the mere act of dying, become wise, tolerant, discreet, modest, truthful or even well-intentioned, if they did not possess those qualities when on earth, and you will be forewarned and forearmed against the shrewd jolts which you are liable to encounter if you approach Spiritualism in too confiding an attitude of mind.

Well, now, you may say: If this subject is beset with such snares and pitfalls that I risk being deceived and there after deceiving others by my experiences, why should I touch it at all? Why not let it alone and trust to the future bringing its own knowledge?" This isn't a bad argument for the intellectually inert or for the morally lazy, but I don't suppose many of my readers come under these headings or they wouldn't be reading this book.

I will give you some reasons why the study of this subject is worthwhile, and well worthwhile, in spite of the possibilities of error.

The first and simplest reason is that you may very possibly be enabled to talk with someone whom you thought you would never see or hear again during the rest of your life. This is the lodestone which has attracted to Spiritualism the majority of its adherents—initially at any rate. Thousands upon thousands have found comfort therein for their bruised hearts; millions will yet find that comfort.

The corollary of this is that we lose all fear of death so soon as we become convinced of the fact of immediate conscious and active survival. We may fear the pain which we fear will accompany death (but which doesn't generally), and we may have an unselfish fear of leaving others behind unprotected and unprovided for, but the fear of that old bogy, Death—so far as he can affect us personally—will disappear.

Now I don't want to be censorious or critical, but this is just about as far as a good many Spiritualists go. If they can get an occasional message from their own special particular people they are perfectly content. They regard the catch phrase "Proof of Survival" as the be-all and end-all of Spiritualism whereas I want to tell them very gently and politely that they are extremely self-centred people, and that "Proof of Survival" is the beginning and not the end of the road.

"What, then, is there beyond?" you may ask. To that I will reply by asking: "Are you satisfied with your religion? Or, if you say that you have no religion, is that because nobody has ever invited you to partake of a religion to which you can accord an intellectual assent? My assertion is that a man who will study what has been made available to us by ancient and modern revelation can build up for himself a picture of the Scheme of the Universe and of the Progress of Humanity, which is perfectly acceptable to a rational intelligence—making allowance, of course, for the fact that there are certain aspects of multidimensional life which are quite outside the scope of our three-dimensional brains.

This is really tremendously important. I don't want to attack the Church. I want this little effort of mine to be positive and constructive. I want to affirm the truth rather than to attack error. I want to applaud the successes of the Church rather than to impeach its failings. But this I must say—the Church's theology and the Church's ideas of the practical details of our future life are quite unacceptable to a mature intellect.

I never initiate an argument on the subject, but I am sometimes attacked by outraged clerics for my published views.

To some of these I have replied by a Shorter Catechism of my own: Do you believe in the Resurrection of the Flesh? Do you believe that people lie unconscious in the tomb awaiting the Day of Judgment? Do you believe in Eternal Damnation for people who for one reason or another never heard of Jesus? For unbaptised babies? For Hindus, Buddhists, Muslims, etc.? For anyone? The answer generally is, "No. I have never taught these things." To which the reply is, "Well then, what do you teach on these subjects?" and the answer is silence.

Now I know perfectly well what almost superhuman courage would be called for if the ecclesiastical authorities decided to face the issue squarely. Once they begin to tinker with the accepted creeds and dogmas, where are they going to stop? They will be up against the Reincarnation issue before they have time to turn round. "Parliament," they will say, "would not allow us to make even a few trivial alterations in the Prayer Book; what would they say if we proposed to dig Anglican Christianity up by the roots?" I think that we must recognise the force of this argument and make up our minds that the stream of clear thinking must come from the outside and not from within the Church.

But the Church, on its part, must realise that the emptiness of its pews is largely a result of this irresolution, and that appeals for the return of its wandering sheep will fall on deaf ears until its professions and its beliefs are made to coincide.

It always seems to me that a man has a right to demand from his religious teachers the fullest obtainable information about the conditions in which he will exist after physical death. It is sheer impertinence to say (as a curate has said to an acquaintance of mine) that such speculation is "morbid and unhealthy." There is, as a matter of fact, an almost embarrassing amount of information available on the subject—embarrassing because much of it is inconsistent and contradictory. But the spice of difficulty should add relish to the task of investigation; it is certainly no excuse for inertia.

The wise man, as I say, will demand to know as much as possible about his future state. If he believes that he will be snuffed out like a candle, he should believe it because he has carefully examined and deliberately rejected the alternatives, and not because it is the most comfortable thing for a selfish materialist to believe.

If and when he accepts the overwhelming evidence that conscious personal existence does continue beyond the grave, he will wish to treat his continuing life as a whole, and modify in thought, word and deed the natural and instinctive expression of his personality so as to accord with a long-term policy, instead of thinking only of the little period which he spends on earth. This is my definition of Religion, and indeed Religion in its widest sense is desperately needed today.

The materialists have had their way with the world, and look where they have led us! We are learning the practical necessity for the Brotherhood of Man, and we are learning the hard way.

To pick up my thread again, I believe that by the study of ancient and modern revelation a sufficiently intelligible picture of the scheme of things can be built up as to serve for a framework for an intelligent man's creed, which in turn can wean his thoughts and actions from the existing almost universal materialism.

There are other aspects of Spiritualism which may or may not be attainable by you if you make it a part of your life. One, of which everyone has heard, but about which most people know very little, is spiritual healing. Most circles which sit regularly are given some of this work to do, but the methods differ very widely and the results cannot be assessed statistically, and so, beyond this mention of the subject, I shall not attempt to deal with it in this little book.

Then there is a vast field of endeavour which is so little known to western humanity that it sounds quite unreal and fantastic. It can't be given a concise name, it is too varied in its nature. Briefly, it consists in cooperation with advanced entities on the other side by contributing an output of power on the earth wavelength to supplement the higher wavelength spiritual power when there is work to be done on earth or in the lower astral planes close to the earth in their rates of vibration. I will give some instances of this later on when I have briefly explained my picture of that tiny fragment of the Cosmic Plan of which I believe that I have a glimmering comprehension, but in its simplest form it has consisted in contributing to the awakening on the other side, of men killed so suddenly in action that they do not realise that they are dead.

Then there is work done in sleep on the astral planes and elsewhere, and finally, there is the straight clerical work of taking down teaching from the beyond, given generally at something beyond dictation speed and involving a desperate effort to keep up.

I shall give some samples of this teaching later on and you shall judge for yourselves of its truth, its beauty and its validity. Our friends wish to be judged by only one criterion: "By their fruits shall ye know them".

THE NATURE OF
MEDIUMSHIP

Now I must devote a little space to an explanation of mediumship, or rather of some of its commonest forms.

The phenomena of mediumship fall into two broad classes: (a) where direct contact is made with the sense recording sections of the medium's brain, those controlling sight, hearing and muscular reactions; and (b) where an artificial and temporary structure of tangible matter is built up from normally intangible ingredients, and communication is effected through that structure.

Under (a) are included seeing or clairvoyance, hearing or clairaudience, automatic writing, trance mediumship, etc., and under (b) materialisation, the direct voice, the levitation of inanimate objects, table-rapping, etc.

This list is in no sense comprehensive. There are many other manifestations of mediumship such as apports (transported matter), spirit photography, inspirational drawing and painting, the production of lights, sounds and perfumes perceptible by non-psychic sitters, and the malicious and destructive manifestations of degraded spirits known as poltergeists, but I cannot deal with all these in the space at my disposal. The point which I want to make is that the phenomena under (b) are the most impressive to the sceptic since they do not (apparently) depend upon the personality of the medium nor are they susceptible to influence by the medium's mentality.

On the other hand these methods are (with the exception of the direct voice) not suitable for the methodical transmission of educational messages, the great bulk of which come through some of the methods mentioned under (a), and so are liable to be tinged by the medium's mentality.

The direct voice is a comparatively rare phenomenon, and, when it does occur, complete darkness is usually necessary for its production. While, therefore, it is technically an admirable method for the transmission of educational material (being free from liability to contamination by the medium's personality), it requires the services of an amanuensis who can keep an accurate record in total darkness.

Some of my own feeble efforts have convinced me how difficult that is. Exceptionally gifted and developed mediums can produce the direct voice in ordinary light, but these are very rare.

(This was written before the tape recorder became generally available).

There is, perhaps, on our part a tendency to overlook the difficulties in communication which exist on the other side. It is comparatively easy for recently departed souls to communicate with earth, since they are still on a wavelength close to ours. Hence the great preponderance of trifling or uninformed messages. But when people who really know the conditions which exist beyond the layers closest to earth wish to speak to us, they may have to "step their communications down" through one or more stages unless they can obtain access to an exceptionally highly developed medium on earth.

You may think that we have enough troubles of our own without worrying about the troubles of those who are trying to communicate with us, but the honest student of the subject will be impressed with the amount of accurate information which reaches us from the other side, and will wish to know as much as possible about the technique so as to be able to form a considered opinion on the validity of any particular message.

The slap-dash and lazy-minded student ignores all the difficulties, and attributes every error to dishonesty on the part of the medium— a grossly unfair attitude of mind.

Personally I regard mediums as a much abused class.

They have a great gift to offer to humanity, if humanity were only capable of recognising the fact. If they use their gifts to earn a livelihood they are called avaricious money-grabbers by censorious Pharisees who trade their own gifts for ten times the price. They are accused of fraud without evidence, and subjected to humiliating and sometimes hurtful restrictions by those whom they are trying to serve.

And yet they continue—Nevertheless, although the overwhelming majority of mediums are thoroughly honest and desire only to give selfless service, they are not always correct in what is transmitted through them—not by any means.

One of the difficulties in the study of the occult is that it is not what we should call an "exact science". That is to say, its phenomena do not lend themselves to precise and tidy classification in accordance with simple rules which we can master with but slight mental effort. As soon as one commits oneself to a generalisation or to the crystallisation of a rule, a great obtrusive exception comes along to reprove our presumption.

There is a comfortable idea that every medium has a doorkeeper, a sort of intangible commissionaire, who vets the list of intending communicators, and chokes off imposters and other undesirables. This may be a general rule for all I know, but if so, it is a rule with many exceptions, or else the commissionaires are not a uniformly competent body of people.

It is no good blinking this fact or pretending that it does not exist. Absolute mental integrity and honesty is essential in these matters. If you are going deliberately to deceive yourself and to push inconvenient facts into the background, as a lazy housemaid sweeps the dust under the hearth rug, you may just as well go back and vegetate in one of the varieties of dogmatic Christianity from which I assume that you are trying to break free, or you wouldn't be reading this book.

On page 124 of my book, *Lychgate,* I stated that at the time of writing, I had had about three dozen letters from relatives of men reported "killed" or "missing, believed killed" telling me that they had had messages through mediums to the effect that their sons or husbands were alive. There was an astonishing similarity in the wording of these messages; once I had started to read one I could almost finish it with my eyes shut.

"Your son is not here, they would say, "he is suffering from head-injuries and has lost his memory. He is being cared for by peasants (or fishermen or monks or whatnot) and he will return safe to you before the roses bloom." Well, by now I have had another couple of dozen of these missives. Some of them may be true; I hope they are, though not one such case has been reported to me; some I know to be false because we happen ourselves to have made contact with the man concerned. Broadly speaking, I believe that they are all false.

Now remember that these messages do not come only from amateur and inexperienced mediums; some of them come through quite well-known people, the average accuracy of whose work is widely accepted.

They do a good deal of harm because, apart from the unnecessary pain which they cause by keeping alive the dying hope of the relatives, they are widely circulated in the first false flush of renewed hope and, when they prove to be false, they arc on record as awful warnings against Spiritualism and are generally ascribed to "fraud" on the part of the medium.

Remember, too, that if I personally have come across about sixty of these messages, their total number probably reaches into thousands, and so the matter is not one that can be brushed aside as being of no importance.

In *Lychgate* I offered three possible reasons which might account for the facts: (a) The idea in the medium's subconscious mind that if she could not contact the missing man it was an indication that he must still be on earth; (b) Some form of thought-transference from the mind of the sitter, desperately anxious that the boy must be alive; and (c) The action of irresponsible personating spirits.

You may perhaps wonder why a circle which believes itself to be in contact with wise and experienced entities should ever be in doubt on a matter of this sort. You might reasonably suppose that any such question had only to be formulated and an immediate answer would be forthcoming.

But that is not the way things happen, at any rate with us.

Things are not made too easy, we have to do the spade work, to ponder and read and reason, and then perhaps we get a little flash of illumination to light us on our way.

Such a hint was given to me in this connection. I was told that the confusion was not always due to "those mischievous ones" but sometimes to desperately lonely souls who will take any chance of making contact with earth where they may be received in a friendly atmosphere. Well, that makes a (d) to add to my (a), (b) and (c), but I don't know that it exhausts the possibilities.

It did help me, however, in another case where a lady wrote to me from America saying that Leslie Howard had sent me a message in cipher (which she enclosed). I replied that Howard was a gentleman when alive and wouldn't have been so uncivil as to send me a lot of gibberish and leave me to try to decipher it. I didn't suppose that he had ceased to be a gentleman because he was dead. I asked her to challenge the communicator in accordance with St. John's formula, "Try the spirits, etc., etc." and see if she couldn't help him to rise superior to such a disreputable occupation.

Some time later I heard that the communicator had survived this test (a point worthy of notice) but had betrayed himself in another way. The self-styled Leslie said that he would bring Raymond Lodge to speak, which he did with apparent success. Unfortunately, "Raymond" in the course of conversion evinced knowledge of something that was known only to "Leslie." Tackled on this point, he broke down and confessed that he was an impostor. "I did it to make you like me," he said.

Readers of *Lychgate* may remember the account on pp. 118 and 119 of the message from an entity claiming to be the first Duke of Wellington, but who had in fact been an Irish dock-labourer.

(I feel a little apologetic for thus referring to my own previous writings, but the alternative is to repeat a good deal of the subject matter of one book in another—a practice which always leaves me with a mild sense of grievance when it is adopted by another author).

I don't want to over-emphasise this question of false messages and impersonating spirits. If I have stressed it at all unduly it is because other writers have sometimes omitted to deal with it altogether; and the result of this is that many inquirers, after a promising start, recoil from the whole subject when they strike one of these "snags." As I have said before, discarnate communication is one of the most valuable methods by which we may attain to hidden truths. If there were some form of celestial censorship which would automatically prevent anything but universal truth from coming over the line, that would be very nice and convenient and would make everything very simple and easy. But there is no guarantee of any such censorship. One of the first truths to be discovered is that nothing should be taken as necessarily true just because it comes from spirit sources. That truth, if assimilated and digested, will form an invaluable starting point in your search for further truth.

WE CAN HELP
THE DEAD

————◆————

Now you may ask, not unreasonably, "Why should I bother about all this? You tell me that the physical phenomena are unimportant and you tell me that the communications may be unreliable. Why should I spend time and trouble in pursuing what may turn out to be only a will-o'-the wisp?" The answer is that if you can get what I have got out of discarnate communication, it will be something that alters your whole view of life and death and life after death. The mere realisation that life and consciousness are continuous on both sides of death is of tremendous importance.

There are many people who believe (or say they believe) that life and existence and consciousness are extinguished forever at physical death. Well, if it is clearly demonstrated to these people that they are wrong, it must have some effect on the way they conduct their lives— or at least one would think so.

The great mass of people probably believe in some vague sort of hereafter. The Church is deliberately woolly on the subject and the ordinary man is not attracted by their anaemic heaven, nor frightened by their eternal hell. Such a system just doesn't make sense to the man in the street, so he is inclined to concentrate on this life which he thinks he knows all about and leave the next life until the time comes to face it.

The result is that when that time does approach the man is frightened. He fears death. And when he wakes up on the other side he often won't believe that he is dead because he feels so much the same as he did before he died.

Others, Christians who have taken their lessons very literally, feel desolate and defrauded because neither Jesus nor any great angel has come to meet them. And the minds of both classes are so confused that those who have come to meet them can't make contact with them. They can't make themselves seen or heard, and so, for a time, these poor souls wander in an earthbound condition until steps can be taken to free them from their disabilities and start them off on the right road.

And there is another thing—you don't even have to believe what I tell you. The mere fact that you have read it with something approaching attention, and let your mind dwell on it as a possibility, will help you. You may "recognise the symptoms," as it were, and realise what has happened when otherwise you would have been lost and bewildered, and you may try to tune yourself in to the wavelength of those who have come to meet you.

I am not going to try in this book to give any extensive picture of the soul's experiences after death; if you want my ideas on that you must read *Lychgate*. What is more, I don't think it matters very much, provided that you will now take it from me that the greatest and most insidious danger to the soul after death is that of stagnation. Especially if you are a lazy type here on earth that work only because you have to in order to obtain the necessities of life. After death you don't suffer from hunger or thirst or exposure.

You don't have to buy clothes or pay rent and rates for your house. You may have earned a good holiday after a long life of labour—well and good, you will get your holiday.

But don't extend it indefinitely. Go back to school and learn about your new life, and, more important still, look round for a job of work helping someone else. Opportunities for either of these activities will not be lacking.

So far the reasons I have given you why you should take a practical interest in this subject have been selfish in so far as I have tried to point out to you the comfort you can gain from renewal of contact with those from whom you have been separated by death, and the advantage which can accrue to your true self from a knowledge of the atmosphere into which you are likely to awaken after death.

Now I want to give you some idea of what Spiritualism in its highest sense means to me.

Has it ever occurred to you that we can help the dead? There are plenty of stories throughout the ages of how angels and spirits have helped us, but precious little the other way round.

I am writing this on Easter Day and in church this morning the congregation said Amen to a prayer by the parson, "For those departed this life in Thy faith and fear." Well, that's all to the good (except that nobody should be taught to fear God, any more than he should be taught to fear his mother); but what about those people who departed this life indifferent or resistant to God? Don't they need our prayers much more than the others? Remember, you don't have to go to church to pray.

You don't even have to go down on your knees. Prayer is only another word for thought. Thought, intense and concentrated. Thought building up a picture in the mind's eye, as detailed and graphic as may be. Thought poured out with all the vigour of your mind and will.

If people could only realise the power of thought, the power of thought to do things, to move mountains, how many of the world's problems would be solved like magic.

Anyhow, that's one way in which we can help—by sending out strong, helpful, constructive thoughts to those who are experiencing the effects of causes which they set in motion during their lifetimes on earth. Not only our friends, but our enemies, too. The veil between the worlds is much thinner than most people realise, and much of the post-war trouble now assailing us is due in some degree to the rage and malice of thousands of hostile souls thrust across the Border with hatred in their hearts and a burning desire for revenge.

Think, too, of the millions of poor creatures, the victims of mass slaughter in concentration camps, reduced by their tortures and sufferings almost to the level of animals before attaining to the release of death. Such as these are bruised and battered in spirit as well as in body and do not recover instantly or without help.

There are those whose duty and whose happiness it is to help these poor souls, but we can make an important contribution to this kind of work on earth or in the unseen regions closest to earth. Remember this, even if you do not quite understand it at the moment, because it is important.

People who are in the 'earthbound' category or lower are quite insensitive to the higher vibrations such as are emitted by the angels and spirits of the higher grades. The latter need a contribution from us for their work—a contribution of good will from our hearts on the low wavelength of earth. It seems an extraordinary thing at first sight, and yet I am constantly coming across fresh instances of it. They say to us, "The redemption of mankind must come through man." You don't have to be a member of a circle or to be an active Spiritualist, in the accepted sense of the word, to make this sort of contribution, but you can, nevertheless, do a lot of good.

Another thing about which strong and concentrated thought desperately needed is the work of the United Nations Organisation and other bodies working for the peace of the world. All such thoughts help and strengthen them, and every defeatist, destructive or cynical thought hurts them and impedes their work.

Perhaps the idea may seem to you quite fantastic that these things should be so, that the influence of discarnate beings should interpenetrate our lives and influence them at every turn, and yet that the curtain between the worlds should be so dense and impermeable to the ordinary man.

It sometimes seems strange to me also, in spite of the numerous personal proofs which I have had that these things are indeed true.

The evidence which has convinced me—which indeed convinced me even before I had any personal experiences of the unseen—is available to anyone who cares to investigate with an open mind.

The explanation is, I think, that this was not always so; it is only in the last sixteen hundred years that orthodox Christianity, philosophy and science, while quarrelling freely with one another, have united to affix the labels of credulity and superstition to a belief in the ever-present circumambient spirit-world in which we live; and western mankind has followed these pastors and masters in the most sheep-like of manners.

How we hate to be thought eccentric, credulous, and different from anyone else! How we cling to outward conformity at least, redoubling our criticism of others in order to bolster up our own flagging agnosticism! How low do we lie, even when convinced against our wills by the weight of the evidence, waiting for the time when the beam will tip, when it will be fashionable to believe and unfashionable to deny! Then will we emerge proudly from our moral funk holes claiming credit for having held these beliefs for years?

I don't think we shall get the credit which we claim—not at any rate in any quarters which really matter—because now is the time when our personal efforts are needed; now during the beam-tipping stage, and not after all the work has been done by other people.

So come out into the open. It doesn't really hurt to be called mad by the people in air raid shelters, believe me.

As I say, you can do a good deal by concentrated collective thought (alias prayer) without making any personal conscious contact with the other side, without joining any circle, and even without ostensibly leaving your entrenched position in the Church or in science or wherever your hole is dug.

It may be, however, that some of you may have the good fortune to be chosen for active work during your lifetime, and so I propose to tell you a little of the kind of work which you may find yourself doing.

But here I want to interpolate a disclaimer. As the result of my former books I have had a good many letters from people in all parts of the country asking me to tell them how to join a circle, as if it were the sort of thing one could do like getting a ticket for a theatre.

Don't ask me this, because I just don't know. Perhaps there are some circles which you can join in this way, but they wouldn't be the sort of circles of which I am thinking.

Don't worry too much about picking and choosing your job. Read the first verse of "Lead Kindly Light" if ever you feel impatient.

To resume; I have described at some length in *Lychgate* the circumstances in which I started active work with my old and new friends and I am not going over all that again.

I have described the various types of work which we have done and have given a fair number of instances. I will give you a few more and then let you know as far as I can how the nature of our work has progressively changed from the "awakening" work which was the commonest type during the war, when casualties were heavy and when the crowds in the astral were continually being reinforced by fresh contingents of men suddenly wiped out of earthly existence and quite unaware of what had happened to them.

What generally used to occur was that we would be sitting in the drawing room of the lady who acted as medium and whom I have designated L.L. for the purpose of these records. All the surroundings would be quite normal in ordinary or artificial light according to the time of year. Then L.L. perhaps would say, "Here are three paratroopers from Normandy," or "Here is the crew of a bomber who think that they have come down in the Ruhr," or something like that, and then would hold them in quiet conversation while those on the other side were working on them to raise their vibrations, and after a bit they would begin to notice something strange in our appearance, something different from themselves, or, by trying to shake hands or to slap me on the back they would discover that we were intangible and the little shock of the discovery would bring realisation, but somehow or other they always eventually tumbled to what had happened, and then they could see the friends who had come to meet them and they would all go off happily together.

Remember that I could never see or hear anything.

I relied on L.L. to tell me what was happening, but when I talked to our visitors they would generally see me and hear me without any intermediary. Daisy, the third member of the circle, was usually present.

28

Here are some instances which have not been previously published. The first happened at Wimbledon on January 20th, 1944, and was recorded from memory the next day.

We had just finished our healing circle when Chang (a Chinese guide) told us that he had someone for us to awaken.

L.L. "It is an American flying boy; he can't see us or anything yet. Will you conduct the conversation? I shall be too far away." (From this point L.L. was in a semi-trance. She spoke with a strong American accent and her face worked in accordance with the emotions of the boy.)

Boy. "Say, what's this? Where am I?"

Self. "It's all right. You have been brought to us so that we may help you."

Boy. "Oh, never mind about me! Help the others— help the others. I've just seen one of them have his leg snapped off by a croc."

Self. "It's all right. The others are being helped. (But he was difficult to pacify. He wanted me to go and help them.) Can you see me now?"'

Boy. "Sure I can see you. But you keep on acting funny; kinda shimmering like a bad movie."

Self. "Yes. I want you to look closely at us and you will see that we do not look solid and real to you. And when you can see that we are not real, then you will be able to see the others who have come to help you."

Boy. "Say, where am I?"

Self. "You are in England."

Boy. "Well, that's a good one! We were flying over -. No, I mustn't tell you, but one of those Japs got us and we couldn't stay in the air."

Self. "You came down out of control?"

Boy. "We were on fire. But we all got out except Tubby. Tubby was in the tail. A dammed death trap that is! Sorry I can't tell you where we were flying."

Self. "Never mind about the Official Secrets Act now; it doesn't affect you any more. I tell you again that this is England—just near London."

Boy. "Say, I've always wanted to visit England, but I never thought it would be like this. But who are you, any way?

Self. "You've been brought to me so that I may help you."

Boy. "Yes, but who are you?"

Self. "Well, you've heard of the Battle of Britain. Did you ever hear of Sir Hugh Dowding?"

Boy. "Why, yes; sure I've heard of him. I know old Dowding."

Self. "Well, I'm old Dowding. I really am. Come on now, put your hand on my shoulder."

Boy. "How can I put my hand on your shoulder when you keep jumping about?" (Of course I hadn't moved).

Self. "All right, then. Smack me on the back. A good hard one."

Boy (tries it and encounters no resistance). "Gosh! Are you a ghost?"

Self. "No, I'm not a ghost."

Boy. "Am I a ghost, then?"

Self. "No. What has happened is that you and I are in different worlds."

Boy. "How do you mean, different worlds? You just said we were both here in England. (Suddenly he realises, and his face puckers up into an expression of agony.) Why, I haven't been all that bad; I don't have to go to hell!"

Self. "No, no, no. You aren't going to hell. We're just trying to wake you up so that you can go and join all your friends."—A pause.

Boy (with a sudden flood of delight). "Why, MAC.

How in hell did you get here? (To me). Will be O.K. now.

Mac's a great guy. Mac taught me to fly." Another long pause, then;

Boy (his face lighting up with indescribable awe, reverence and joy. Speaking very slowly). "Today shalt thou be with Me in Paradise. Well, I'm no worse than the thief, and I guess I will be. (He talks to Mac for a little, then—) Say, I understand now. Mac got his too. (See's Tubby).

Why, Tubby, how did you get here?" Tubby (apparently so called because he is very tall and extremely thin). "We're all here. We've been here all the time, but we couldn't see one another nor see you; we could only hear your voice." (Now they can all see one another and are talking together.)

Chang. "Will you tell me what is the quality of the men who sit in front of your flying birds? Are they the leaders? Are they in command?"

Self. "Yes. They are called the pilots. They control the aeroplane. When they pull the stick the nose goes up and when they push it the nose goes down. They steer to right or left with their feet."

Boy (breaking in). "Yeah, and when you go like this, damn all happens. (Frantic movements of the stick indicating being shot down out of control.)

Chang. "What is this name, Mac? There are many so-called here. Oh! He is telling me that it is only a part of a name."

Self. "Yes, and there are a good many Changs in China." Chang (smiling). "That is so." The boy was a youngster, not more than about 20, with a round baby face, straight fair hair and very blue eyes. They all went off happily together.

About the next case I have only a few disjointed notes.

It was on 3rd February 1944, and the "patient" was the pilot of a bomber shot down in flames over Berlin.

At first he thought he was still in the plane, pushing, pushing, pushing to get his wounded navigator through the escape hatch.

Then when his mind became a little clearer, he thought that he was in Germany being examined by a Nazi intelligence officer, and he would not speak or answer any questions. I tried to reassure him by telling him who I was, but he only said, "Oh, yeah, and I'm Cunningham, the famous sailor!" He said that I couldn't be Dowding because I was not in uniform. Then he started cross-examining me, and asked, "How would you get out of a burning plane?" I told him, and he said, "Um, you seem to know your stuff." Finally he began to see a bit better, and as he looked at me he said ruminatively and without intention of giving offence, "He might be at that—I know his ugly mug." At last he saw something invisible to us and said, "Lead kindly light, amid the encircling gloom. Lead Thou me Home" After which he went off quite contentedly with Clarice who had assumed the appearance of a Red Cross nurse for the occasion.

(Clarice is my wife who is a very active member of our group. She died in 1920.) A voice is heard saying, "Greater love hath no man than this, that he lay down his life for his friend." After the healing circle on March 30th, 1944, James (who commanded a squadron in the Battle of Britain) says: "We have a crew for you to wake up. It shouldn't be a difficult job. My heart is very much in this because some of my friends are among them. They are not here yet: as a matter of fact they are walking along the road outside. They will come in here."

L.L. "Here they are, seven of them. The leader seems to be a squadron leader with fair, wavy hair. Now they are looking at a big picture on the wall. They can't see us yet.

They think they are in Germany. One of them says: They seem to be quite civilised people here. I mean to say, this is a very nicely furnished and homelike room.'" They move over to the piano. One of them wishes to play. I say, "You won't be able to open it," and I go across and open the piano.

L.L. "He didn't like that! He says, gosh, this house must be haunted.' "She describes some other members of the crew, a ginger haired lad and a little dark Jewish-looking boy.

Now they are beginning to see us. They can't understand the new dimensions. With ten people in it the room ought to be crowded, but it doesn't seem to be. Five of them are sitting on the music seat, meant to accommodate two. Now the leader begins to talk to me. He says, "How is it that you are talking English?"

Self. "Because I am English."

Leader. "Where are we, then?"

Self. "This is Wimbledon, do you know it?"

Leader. "I should just say I do!"

Self. "All right, then. You have just been walking along the Worple Road."

Leader. "But how did we get here? We must have come down over the Ruhr."

Self. "You have been brought here that we may help you."

Leader. "But who are you?" I go to the mantelpiece, take down a picture of myself in uniform, and hold it beside my face.

Self. "Do you know who I am now?" Yes. They all recognised me now. One says, "I remember you when you came to inspect us at Biggin Hill."

Leader. "How can you help us?"

Self. "Oh, just by talking to you and helping you to realise your position. Do you see me clearly? Do I look natural?"

Leader. "Yes, of course you do."

Self. "Very well, then. Shake hands." (I hold out my hand.)

Leader. "I can't get hold of it. Why don't you grip my hand?"

Self. "All right, I will. Watch very carefully" (and I slowly close my hand through his without his feeling anything).

L.L. "He didn't like that!" Just then the dark lad comes up behind and gives me a terrific smack on the back. He utters a shrill Cockney yelp as his hand encounters no resistance.

Leader. "Look here, Sir, are you trying to tell us that we are—that this is death?"

Self. "Yes. That is exactly what I have been trying to get you to realise.'

Leader. "But how can we be dead? We are just as we were before."

Self. "Yes. Now you can see what a ridiculous little barrier death is. This death of which everyone is so frightened (Now he can see James. I introduce them.) Talk to him and he will be able to explain much more than I can." The tail gunner says: "I remember a Hun fighter coming up behind and knowing that something was going to happen. Then I remember no more until we were on the road outside." James explains that they were all blown to pieces instantaneously in their aeroplane three or four days previously, over the Ruhr.

Now they can see all their other R.A.F. friends who have come to meet them and they all go off together.

May 11th, 1944.

L.L. "They have got an airman. He is asleep. A huge person. Send out love; think him awake. He is stirring —waking up. He has the bluest of blue eyes. Now he sees the boys around him and he sees us, too. James is talking to him and pointing out the difference in appearance between them and us. Then come two other boys, they are whistling and quite happy. They can't see us or anybody at the moment.

They are in the Fleet Air Arm, one fair and the other darker. One has three bands on his sleeve, the other only one band. Now they see us."

Commander. " Excuse me, can you tell me where we are? "

Self. "Yes. This is Wimbledon." (But he doesn't take it in).

Commander. " How extraordinary to find English people about!"

Self. "Why? What did you expect to see?"

Commander (viciously). "Little yellow devils!" After satisfying himself of my identity he explained that he thought they were coming down in the sea.

Self. "Yes. You did come down in the sea, and while you were unconscious you were brought back here."

Commander. "Trust the Navy! Where would you be without the Navy? "

Self. "Where would you be without us? "

Commander. "Oh, well, I daresay it's about 50/50." Self. "But the Navy didn't bring you here."

Commander. "What? The underground movement operating over all that distance. What a show!"

Self. "Well, I shouldn't exactly call it an underground movement. Overground might be a better word." Now the youngster whose name is Rory has been thinking and suddenly he knows.

Rory. "Are you trying to tell us that we've passed out?"

Self. "Yes, we are on different planes of existence now. Slap me on the back and see what happens."

Rory (to the Commander). "No, you do it." He does so and his hand goes through me. Now they both realise.

Commander. "It's like going to bed in one hemisphere and waking up in another. (They are beginning to see James and the boys). It's the strangest thing out. Here today and gone tomorrow; you never know where you'll land." They are shaking hands with James and the other pilots.

The blue-eyed giant turns out to have been their navigator.

Commander. "Well, have you got your charts for this new voyage?" James is making the "operation finished" signal and then "thumbs up." (The word Penang was repeated three different times).

May 22nd, 1944.

L.L. "Here are two R.A.F. boys wearing 'Mae West' jackets. One has hurt his ankle and is nursing it. He is very dark, with a black moustache. The other, very fair, is smoking a cigarette. The dark one is cursing freely; his companion says: 'Stow it. Come on. Lean on me. Hop a bit and see where we can get to.'" "Here are two more coming along. One is a tiny Cockney."

The Fair One. "Where is Galbraith? "

The Tiny One. "We can't find him."

The Fair One. "The deuce we can't. He is the only one likely to know where we are."

The Tiny One. "I think I know where we are. I think we are in Germany. Look, the river isn't far away, but we can't have been over here very much, there's not enough damage." Now the fair one has seen us.

The Fair One. "I don't understand this. One moment we are out of doors and the next we are in a house."

The Dark One. "I don't care. Here's a chair." (Sits down). " They can all see us now." The Tiny One. "Wait a minute. I'll try and find out what the old chap's writing."

Self. "Yes. Come and have a look over my shoulder."

The Fair One. "Just a moment. You are speaking English. Can you tell us where we are?"

Self. "You are in Wimbledon."

The Fair One. "Will you help us to get back?"

Self. "Where do you want to go? " (But they won't tell me for Security reasons).

Self. "As a matter of fact I know where you want to go"

The Fair One. "It's strange, but I don't want to move." They go on asking after Galbraith, who was their navigator. I ask L.L. "Is James there? James, what happened to Galbraith?"

James. "Galbraith baled out." (I tell them this).

The Tiny One. "That's a good joke! What should he want to bale out for? Nothing happened to us. We're all right." James explains that the machine blew up. It was blown into halves. Galbraith was able to escape by parachute.

They overhear but don't understand.

Self. "Galbraith got away with it, but you four didn't."

The Fair One. "What do you mean? We're here all right."

Self (to Tiny). "Give me a smack on the back, will you?"

The Tiny One. "Watch me! " (Tries). " Oh, you're made of India rubber, are you? " (Tries again).

The Fair One. "Stop it now! Yes, thanks, I see."

The Tiny One (dancing about). "We're spooks, we're spooks, we're spooks!" They begin to see us looking shimmery and unreal. I tell them to look round and I tell them who James is. They see him.

The Fair One (saluting James). "Reporting for duty, Sir." Now they see all the great crowd of the Boys.

The fair one can't see me any more, but thanks us nicely.

He says: "There's nothing to worry about. We're exactly as we were."

The Tiny One. "If we're spooks, Tyndall's leg isn't broken, is it? "

Self. "No. He will find he can use it if he tries."

The Tiny One. "Go on, then. Get up, you lazy lump!"

The Dark One (recognising a friend). "Why, hullo Bill! You see we couldn't let you fellows steal a march on us. We've caught up—we've caught up!" Now, I shouldn't like anyone to get the idea this is the only way in which these lads are awakened to their new life, or that we are the only operators of this particular method.

Quite a number of people are engaged in this work, but for some reason or other it is very little known. Also you must remember that every little drama, such as I have described, is watched by numbers of unseen spectators who see what is happening and apply the illumination to their own conditions.

There is another aspect to these activities: I believe that they are arranged to some extent for our own education. Anyhow, our work never seems to get into a groove: so soon as we become accustomed to one form of activity the nature of the work changes and we find ourselves doing something else.

I think that one of the most important activities of our circle is the receipt of instruction; samples of which I propose to give now. 'Z' is the communicator, and, if I say that he is an Egyptian, I mean only that he manifests most frequently in that form. He has belonged to Egypt, but to other countries also in his time. However, it is not so much what 'Z' is but what he says, that is important.

Here follow five of his talks, with the dates on which they were given. At the end of each I have appended one of the blessings with which he normally closes our circles.

I hope that this will introduce no incongruity, but I want to give a few samples of what is one of the most attractive features of our sittings.

MAN'S CRYING NEED

4th July, 1945

The world today, more than at any other time in its chequered history, needs a guiding star, a vision, a hope.

War, with its attendant discomforts, its physical horrors and mental tortures, can be a power for the growth and development of man, or a power for the annihilation of all that part of him which makes life manifest to him beyond the level of blind, unreasoning instinct, as is the case with animal and plant and mineral life.

Evolving life must struggle always; there must be effort for any lasting progress. Yet man is turning his back on this basic truth—a truth which he will ignore at his peril.

On all sides one hears of schemes where initiative will be taken away, where effort will be nullified. All such schemes are doomed to failure because they go against the very fundamentals of life itself. But before they fail they will have destroyed much that is valuable and almost irreplaceable.

The scheme of the Universe provides that human life must evolve. The environment of this Universe is confined by the fact that life must evolve through effort. Not a strained, painful effort, but a natural growth brought about by the order of law which says that all effort shall bring greater understanding and greater opportunities.

That the efforts of the few shall be all that is necessary to bring about the salvation of the many is a pernicious doctrine.

The efforts of the few can at best only hold at bay the appalling disasters which the apathy of the many naturally attracts.

But a society based on this futile doctrine of allowing a group or a government to do for the people these things which the people must do for themselves, is doomed to eventual extinction. The first and last reason for the existence of life on this planet is that individual Monads* may penetrate into its gloom and refine and elevate it.

To do this it is necessary for the human forms hiding the Monadic glow to work ceaselessly to clear the way.

Every individual incarnate has a right to the opportunity to do this very thing. No one individual is privileged above another, except by the greater vision that his own efforts have engendered in him. And that vision brings the responsibility to help others less evolved, not to remove the boulders from the path, but to throw some light so that they may be seen more clearly.

In removing the boulders much superfluous weight and flabbiness is cast aside—the effort calls forth a ray of divine power, and no one

---

* The highest part of Self, which inhabits the regions of pure Spirit.

has the right to refuse this ray to another by completing for him the task he should tackle for himself.

Respect for himself, that he will be independent yet gentle of spirit; respect for his fellow creatures, that he will concede to them the rights and privileges he wishes to enjoy himself (and this means to all classes of society, respect for the life flowing around him in every form, so that he will hesitate to destroy), that is the keynote for the new age.

To gain this respect what must man do? Physically he must be healthy—that means good food, clean habitations and living, exercise and rest.

Mentally he must be alert-that means learning, learning by books, learning by listening to others and learning by experimenting and experiencing for himself.

Spiritually he must be aware—that means that he must realise and accept the Immanence of God in himself and all his fellow creatures. That he must remember that he is greater than all the temptations which beset him. That he must differentiate between religion and true spirit, that he must be prepared by unremitting effort to enjoy to the full the world God has given to him and which he is making— not God—man is creating the earth conditions. That he must have dignity and justice for himself and that he may recognise it for others.

These things he can accomplish by meditation and prayer —meditation on the life of One who led the way and prayer which is a living life.

Today the earth needs more than ever hope and vision; and these man can have, for the course of evolution is sure, and some there are who, seeing the vision, are helping evolution along.

But the vision can only be realised when each individual accepts his responsibility and works physically, mentally and spiritually with continuous effort and unremitting labour, one to help the other, to treat with courtesy even his enemies, and with respect those with whom he deals.

With love to all in his heart what man can fail to see and follow the vision of heaven on earth?

Blessing.

And now may His blessing rest upon you all.

May you go forward strong in His work. May you be deemed worthy to feel His presence and be glorified therein.

And unto Him shall all men aspire, and unto Him shall be brought all who are weak, all who labour and all who sorrow, that He may take them in His arms and bring them peace. *Amen.*

THE PROBLEM OF PAIN

—————◦●◦—————

6th July, 1945

On the long journey of life the soul experiences much that is disappointing and painful. It is difficult to see through the haze of deceit and horror to the still peace of the divine plan. Yet it is a truth that behind the maze of suffering and ugliness is the quiet glow of the beauty to be made manifest. Truth is beautiful—make no mistake about that. Truth is hidden behind ugliness and malformation.

Truth leads to happiness and to joy that is not understandable until it is experienced.

Many men teach and believe that sorrow and pain and misery are necessary parts of the evolutionary plan. That is not true. They are necessary only so long as man wills them to be so. You will reply that men learn by suffering, that in these last years the people who suffered became more kindly with one another, more thoughtful, more considerate, while those who were removed from the scenes of horror and destruction remain self-absorbed and wrapped up in their little world. No doubt this is a truth, for humanity is young and weak. But is this the only way to teach tolerance and pity and love. Must you have destruction of life and beauty of form, and horror indescribable, to learn to love your neighbour as yourself? Surely man is not so vile that there is no better way! The way of the divine plan does not include that kind of suffering. Man ordained that. So soon as man realises this truth so soon will he take up his responsibility and take the necessary steps to reduce this great sorrow of humanity.

Make no mistake—the ways of living for mankind are man's responsibility.

War is not a necessary part of the discipline, neither is famine nor disease. These come about because of the abuse by man of the universal laws and because of man's ignorance of the universal laws.

What are the causes of war? A few inflated egos, drunk with a vision of power, can cause war. A few self-seeking economists, by diverse means, can cause war. A few undisciplined, unscrupulous dreamers can cause war. A few! How is it that only a few can cause so much sorrow and pain? Because men still keep their heads bent and their eyes lowered as they did in the time long past when a two-dimensional world was all they knew.

Men still believe that to gain happiness and freedom from fear and pain all that is necessary is to have worldly success.

Then give a man all he needs of the world's goods. Give to him a healthy body, warm and lovely clothing, a spacious and beautiful home, exercise to amuse him and appetising food to satisfy his hunger. What then? Is he happy? These things are the birthright of all men. There are enough fruits of the earth for all to enjoy. Man must learn how to garner them to the best advantage of all, not the few.

But if all men were freed from the grind of poverty, the threat of disease and hunger, would war cease? No, a thousand times no, for economic reasons alone do not cause war.

There is a further aspect of man besides the physical body. The body is the temple of the spirit, and as such it is the duty of every man to tend and care for it, to feed and cleanse it, to exercise and rest it, as he would a valuable animal.

But there is a greater need in man than the need of physical comfort and well-being. The mental capacity of man is expanding and growing, and he seeks ever-new fields of exploration and endeavour.

Many there are whose mental growth is negligible, and already the seeds show that this is recognised by man. In schemes for education the first fruits are showing. It is thought, and rightly, that all men are entitled to the growth which education brings. But education is a two-edged sword. It can throw open the doors to untold vistas of vision and understanding, or it can throw open the doors to the narrow antechamber of power and intellectual pride. Man must learn the balance between the two. Given these two gifts, physical and mental satisfaction, is he happy? Is there not some other tug at his heartstrings, some restless urge driving him—whither? Truly man cannot live by bread alone. Give him all the fruits of the earth, all the treasures of the intellect, and still he hungers.

Man is a threefold being and must be developed as a trinity.

Ignore the body and you have disease and pain.

Ignore the intellect and you have sorrow and blind lusts.

Ignore the Spirit and you die.

The third aspect which moulds and holds the other two must now come into its own. No longer can man scorn it, no longer ignore it as a poor relation is ignored.

The laws of the Universe are the laws of the Spirit.

These laws are known to the spirit incarnate in each individual. The unfolding of this knowledge is the task of all and, as it unfolds, the laws will operate in harmony, for harmony is the keynote of the Universe, and in harmony are beauty and love and joy. That is the heritage of man— his true birthright—not war and destruction and suffering.

The suffering of the mystic is not understandable by one who has not unfolded the depths within himself. It is the suffering of nature as she changes form; a sadness for what is past, but with hope for the future to balance it—the exquisite sadness sheer beauty brings—the sadness of joy which bursts the bonds of self and throws open the doorway of growth.

This is the suffering of which mystics speak, and which man in his misunderstanding has accepted as physical and mental suffering.

Throw off the bonds of sentimental thought, of craven fear, and stand upright! Demand your birthright for yourself and for your fellows. Set the spirit free in its earthly confine of material form. Accept its gift of joy and vision —laugh and sing, be happy, for the ultimate working out of the law is sure. Start its unfoldment on the way, begin now with yourself, and look outward and upward to see the design, and inward to realise its power and glory. For the heritage of man is unity with the divine, and divinity permeates all.

Blessing

Eternal Spirit, open Thou the gateway of understanding. Let Thy hand take Thy children through. Let Thy strength encourage them. Let Thy love enfold them, that they may carry out Thy desire and fulfil Thy plan concerning them. And unto Thee we bring our gifts of love, our adoration, and our tasks well or ill done. *Amen.*

WORLD CHAOS

13th July, 1945

The problem of world chaos is linked very closely with the chaos in the mind of humanity. Man insists on looking outward for causes instead of looking inward.

As with the individual, so with a nation. An individual who has an unquiet spirit will have an unquiet environment.

Take any day of your own personal life and look closely to see the truth of this. When peace reigned within, all disturbances from without were unable to disturb and gradually as the hours advanced the outward chaos disappeared. Similarly on a day when tumult and discord held the spirit, though the environment were peaceful, unless a determined effort were made, storms arose and strife and chaos reigned outwardly also, one discord attracting another until you are glad to retire to rest and refresh the spirit in the healing atmosphere of the wider world.

So it is with nations. A nation is made up of individuals. If the number of selfless, aspiring individuals outnumbers the selfish, egocentric individuals, then the life of the nation will flow in accord with the creative stream.

Where the larger number stand for progress and unity, and respect the individual life-spark and seek to have it develop, then the grit of the few will be swept onward also, with but an odd eruption which will not alter the main course of events.

Where the many are seeking only for self, where those who are privileged to use power and strength abuse that privilege; where those who, seeing this abuse, yet are not sufficiently stirred to clear the grit away or at least to make a stand against it, then disaster in one form or another inevitably follows. The grit accumulates, the stream flows and spreads until it bursts all bounds—then a nation suffers.

And, if it is to suffer until the last piece of grit is cleared away, then it is blessed.

Take the nation you have in mind,* study its history, study it deeply—weigh the progress and advancement, weigh the spiritual life, weigh the sorrow and neglect of the many.

See which side the scales weigh heaviest; it will be more than surprising if you do not find the law working.

Outwardly it seems many innocent people suffer but the inner life is not revealed to you.

---

* Germany was on my mind.

But let us consider only the outward semblance. Who is to blame for the innocent sufferer? You, my friend, you and all the others of your times who do not interest yourselves. How can you be blamed for things of which you were ignorant? Did you try to illumine your ignorance? Did you open your consciousness to the wider fields beyond your own hearth and your own circle of friends? Interference? No, you cannot interfere in the affairs of another, but it is possible to tackle gently an obvious evil.

That you realise the evil is there is a step in the right direction. Then hold in your mind the positive negation of that evil. Think of it as removed and replaced by good.

If the opportunity for action on the physical plane comes to you, as come it will if your aims are sincere, then, by the very act of will you have been practising, you will have at your command the forces of light.

Keep your mind wide open and perform diligently the tasks of every day. See to it that harmony reigns in your immediate surroundings—teach others to do the same. Let the gospel of harmony spread, and gradually that peace and felicity of which you dream will become a fact.

Blessing.

And now let us praise Him to whom we owe all that we have. Let us give thanks for all that we are and all that we shall become. Let us make ourselves worthy instruments in His service and rededicate ourselves to Him. Let His love surround us, His blessing rest upon us. *Amen.*

THE LOWER SELF

20th July, 1945

The lower self may mean many aspects of the human side of man. There is that aspect which appertains to the animal instincts—a very familiar lower self to many.

It is a mistake, I think, to try to separate the selves—they interpenetrate each the other and grow and develop almost simultaneously. At least that is the wisest growth.

Sometimes, of course, a rapid advancement is made in one particular direction, and to keep the balance even it is best, when this occurs, to pause long enough for the other sides of one's nature to catch up. Often this catching up occurs in another experience of life, in the "cabbagey" existence one meets. Then the balance is being readjusted so that no harm may ensue.

But there is an aspect of the lower self known to the mystic which must be eliminated. It is not easy clearly to define this state.

Perhaps it could be best explained in this way. When the personality has garnered all its experience for this cycle then it takes its sheaves to the threshold of the Sanctuary, there to make offering if the time is ripe.

Here on the threshold it gleans over the sheaves and sometimes it happens that they become very dear to it and there is a struggle to assess each one at its proper value. It is this struggle of the personality which is called the sublimation of the lower self, when the personality is lost completely in the merging into the wider consciousness.

Many times it happens that the dweller on the threshold is not ready for the gleaning. The sheaves may be few—or perhaps held too dear. Then the sublimation cannot occur.

The struggle may be long drawn out or sharp and short, but it is one to which we all must come at one time or another.

Do not despise the lower self—even that lowest aspect —the animal aspect. It teaches much and learns much and under the control of the true self is the ballast and the strength of the whole. Without it chaos reigns, with it out of control there is disaster.

Know it, make it accept its proper place in the scheme and harmony will be the result: harmony in living—the heritage of all.

Blessing (through Chang this time).

Let His blessing rest upon you and refresh you as the rain refreshes the thirsty earth. Let His power flow through you as the wind blows over the great wastes of earth, carrying the seeds for new forests. Let

His power uphold you as the mountains rise majestically in strength,
firm and strong and enduring.

Let Him dwell within your hearts as the shrine within the temple.

May you walk in His ways. *Amen.*

THE LAST ENEMY

20th July, 1945

The last enemy—death? Many people think of death thus, but death is not the last enemy to be fought and conquered. Death is in reality a friend who bursts the bonds of physical matter and opens the gateway to the great vistas of life. What makes death, the great friend, appear an enemy to man? That real last enemy which, subtle and strong, hides in every crevice—fear. Fear distorts and destroys. Fear is with man from the beginning, twisting and discolouring, misrepresenting and distorting, until the real is lost in a fog of doubt and bewilderment.

Man fears fire and water and air; he fears the tempest; he fears nature; he fears poverty; he fears disease; he fears his fellows; he fears himself.

Fear is the destroyer—the greatest enemy. How is he to be vanquished? Knowledge is the weapon. To understand is to cast out fear. You cannot be afraid of that which you truly understand, for understanding leads to love, and love is the strongest thing in the universe. Love conquers fear.

To understand the laws of nature brings awe and wonder to man. When he understands his fellows he has tolerance and sympathy. Knowledge of self brings liberation and love.

To conquer fear then man must seek diligently. He must not only learn the laws of nature, he must learn to bring his own life into harmony with these laws. He must learn the laws governing the life of man himself: the various forms the life-energy uses to experience life in the material world.

Man is made of more than physical atoms. A study of his composition will bring wonders undreamed of to his ken.

A fascinating adventure opens out before him when he embarks on the study of the being who was created by the Creator of all things, in His own image.

Do you think of this Creator as a being of flesh and blood only? Can you circumscribe Him thus? If not, then must you meditate upon His nature, and to understand Him you much first understand yourself.

In the world today men are weary and seek some alleviation from the burden of birth. The task is easier than they know, the way open and clear before them, yet they hesitate, blind and doubting, seeing only the distortion of fear.

The remedy for the ills of the world lies with man himself and this truth cannot be spoken too often or too loudly. Man ever seeks to find a scapegoat—the shame in himself for his failure makes him turn outwards in censorious mood. As it is with nations, so with the individual— when you blame, are you certain there is no blame in yourself? When you condemn are you faultless? Yet you must not condone that which is evil. How then must you act? In your individual and personal relations cultivate understanding and tolerance, search your own heart before you pass judgment. Here is a very simple and easily understood injunction, familiar to you all; take it from its dusty shelf, burnish it up and hold it continuously before your eyes that you may not forget it: Do unto others as ye would be done by. Succinct? Clear? Yes. Capable of misrepresentation? No. You cannot evade truth, turn and twist it as you will. Truth confronts you still.

Take this injunction and live by it and it will bring to you knowledge from the fountain of the Most High, for in living the law of harmony you will attract that law to yourself. No longer will you fear nature or poverty or hunger; no longer will you fear death, for you yourself will be Alive.

Blessing

And now call on the love ray and send it out over this sad dark star, and let the love of the Most High drench and purify every darkest corner of the earth plane.

Let the light from the Holy of Holies shine forth in brilliance. Let fear stumble and die. Let hope rise triumphant. Let hatred fade away in the blinding glory of His everlasting day, and in His keeping may we walk in peace. *Amen.*

NOW you may perhaps say: "Who are these Egyptians and Chinese and ancient bodies in general who speak to us? With what authority do they speak, and why should we pay any attention to them?" If you are a clergyman you will almost certainly ask this, and you may very probably ask it if you are a layman.

The answer is, I think, that they are "Men of good will." Men who finished with the necessity of inhabiting a body of flesh hundreds or thousands of years ago. Men who might have pursued their way far into the realms of bliss if they were not held back by a consuming love for poor humanity. The Christian is supposed to believe the pronouncement, "He shall give His angels charge over thee to keep thee in all thy ways, and in their hands shall they bear thee up lest thou dash thy foot against a stone" but that is not usually one of the extracts from holy writ which he considers as applicable to his daily life.

And yet it is applicable.

I will never say that with God anything is impossible, but some things are much more probable than others; and to me it seems much more improbable that the central authority should attempt to operate the universe single-handed than that He should organise it under central control but with delegated authority.

Anyhow, I believe that one of the most important changes which is shortly due to be brought about in the religious outlook of the Western Hemisphere is a recognition of the influence on our lives brought to bear by the saints and angels, by the spirits and souls of the righteous, yes, and by the spirits and souls of the unrighteous too. It is all quite logical; if you accept the influence for good of the children of light, you should not ignore the influence for evil of the children of darkness.

Not that any soul remains permanently in the darkness.

It is an integral part of my faith that every soul will eventually come to complete happiness and perfection, but the way to the light leads sometimes through dark places when that is the deliberate choice of the soul.

And it isn't only on the lives of individuals that discarnate spirits exercise their influence, national deliverances and disasters are effected by their agency and according to their nature. I say in all seriousness that the rise to temporary power and the subsequent downfall of Germany in the recent war was due to her deliberate and conscious alliance with the powers of darkness. Black Magic is not dead. The ordinary man's scepticism and materialism has helped it to conceal its existence of recent years; but it remains a major danger to the peace and progress of the world. For Black Magic may be defined as the misuse of spiritual power for worldly and selfish ends.

And so, for the purpose of my developing argument, I should like you provisionally to accept the idea that there is a vast number of discarnate souls eager and anxious to instruct humanity. The majority of these never get farther than the wishing stage because they fail to find intermediaries in the shape of mediums.

Of the successful ones a large proportion have started to broadcast before they know what they are talking about (because freewill is a law of the universe and operates indifferently on both sides of the grave), there is a certain proportion of mischievous ones who deceive deliberately, and a further proportion of lonely souls, attracted to the medium like the moth to the candle, ready to adopt any pose if only they be received with friendliness.

Add to all this that progressed spirits often pour their wisdom into the ears of listeners who make no attempt to publish the messages beyond the confines of their own little circle (and sometimes don't even keep notes), and you will see what a problem confronts the spirit world in getting true teaching through to humanity.

The difficulty doesn't even end there, because there is no generally accepted acid test to which messages can be subjected as a check to their accuracy.

Each recipient sticks up loyally for his own patrons.

I uphold 'Z' and Chang as paragons of wisdom and truth, but other people, who have received different teaching, maintain the reliability of their own prophets with equal assurance and certainty.

That's what makes it all so difficult, and that's what makes it all so interesting. I have been told several times: "Accept all inspiration gratefully, but accept nothing because it comes from spiritual sources. Accept only that which your spirit knows is of God." And again: "We would ask you to keep before you as you go forward the rule: What the reason cannot accept, think over well. What the intuitive power cannot accept, reject." I suppose that I haven't been very successful yet in developing my intuition. Anyway, I seem to make a good many mistakes.

It always seems to me that we human beings accept very casually the ministrations of those who are trying to help us (when we do not ignore them altogether).

Our helpers are very patient, but even they are sometimes moved to remonstrance by our attitude.

On pages 119 and 120 of *Many Mansions* I quoted some general criticisms from R. J. Lees's book, *Through the Mists*, and Vale Owen's Zabdiel who says: "For the rest, we do not go on bended knee. That let them also keep in mind. We do not proffer gifts as slaves to princes." Last August even the courteous and good-tempered Chang felt that a protest was overdue. We had been discussing the (to us) strange circumstance that the Great Ones should have need of our earth-vibrations as a contribution to their work. Chang said: "Why is that such a strange thought? Can't you realise that here and now you are part of the whole? Your world is not separate from the other; it is part and parcel of it now. Between the highest sphere and earth there are repercussions. We are not altruistic altogether; we are wearied by many repercussions from earth which we dislike.

"When the earth is at peace (an utterly unknown state of affairs), but when there has been a large area of the earth at peace, at such times as your festival of the birth of the Christ-child, when millions of people are thinking in love, mostly of their own little circle, but in many cases love extends beyond the immediate surroundings and embraces even unknown people; then the vibratory note of earth is clear and melodious. The discordant note of the warring few is overcome by the positive note of the loving majority so that the little discord fades not unpleasantly into the great chord of the universe."

At such times the depths of the deepest man-created hell disgorge those who are striving (and all are striving), and every living being is raised one step nearer fulfilment.

"Then do we, honourable souls, miserably unworthy though we are, become free to go about our own business and we taste the joys of Buddhi*—the joys of Heaven—the great indescribable emotion of utter fulfilment and a complete polarity. Such moments alas are miserably few; our honourable brethren on the ear much prefer the separate idea of being the chosen creatures of the Creator, than which there is none higher.

"Oh, miserable worms that grovel in the earth! Oh, dishonourable sons of honourable mothers! Such pride and selfishness guide your footsteps that ye dare make your casket black as ebony, catching but little reflection from its inner reality.

"So it is because of the lustful prides of the wretches called men that the liberated spirits are held on the wheel and labour to bring an inkling of their true destiny to the separate ones. It is a sad business; yet we accept our task —for alack, but yesterday we also were miserable worms grovelling in the earth, blind and unthinking, and we are but little better today. Z. "So, my honourable friends, bear with Chang when he reminds you of your wretched origins." Pretty straight from the shoulder, what! Now perhaps another thing has

* One of the higher spheres.

struck you—the basically "Christian" language in which these messages are couched.

I am not sure, but I don't think that either Z or Chang had a chance of being a Christian when on earth, because I don't think that either has been in incarnation since the time of Jesus. But the point that I wish to make is that the Christ Spirit is not the exclusive property of us who have the temerity to call ourselves Christians. It has permeated every important religion since the beginning of time. True, the Christ Spirit overshadowed Jesus during His ministry on earth, but it has also overshadowed other Great Ones in the past; and He will come again, perhaps once, perhaps more than once: who can see into the great Plan of Evolution? I think that we should even be guilty of undue arrogance if we were to claim the Christ Spirit as being exclusively concerned with the earth in His manifestations in matter.

However this may be, the injunctions "Love thy neighbour as thyself" and "Do as you would be done by," are not the exclusive property of Christians. They are the foundation stones of all religions, buried though they may have been by the venality of priests or by the indifference of the laity.

We have achieved an uneasy equilibrium of personal conduct in civilised and law-abiding countries. It is obviously inconvenient to the great majority of the population that thieves and murderers should operate unchecked, and so, over a long period, a code of laws, and a police force and judicature to enforce those laws have been built up.

My point is that within a nation we, although far from perfect morally, can achieve tolerable living conditions because of a code of laws generally agreed and impartially enforced.

Between nations, however, there is neither adequate morality nor any agreed code of behaviour: and this seems to me to be the weakness of all systems of international organisation hitherto devised.

In the absence of such a code, agreed, accepted, and enforced, the national thief and the national murderer can operate whenever he feels himself strong enough to do so.

All talk of international police and an international judiciary is hot air unless and until an international code of conduct is universally accepted as a basis for universal international law. Personally, I don't think that a successful international control based on force is ever likely to materialise. I think that the solution will lie in more spiritual methods. But that is only a personal opinion. What sticks out a mile is that nuclear fission has now given men the opportunity to destroy one another's lives and property on such a scale that organised civilisation is unlikely to survive its general application as a method of war. And so perhaps, if men's hearts cannot be turned by love alone, the sight of the abyss which yawns before their feet may have a moderating influence on their conduct.

The above divagation into the field of international politics is not wholly irrelevant, because I want to say that the condition of the earth, the outcome of the war, the Indian problem, the conditions in European countries and in China and the progress of the United Nations

Organisation, are all matters which very clearly interest and concern progressed and powerful spirits.

I know little of their methods, and that little comes under the heading of the "hidden work," but the broad law seems to be that direct interference is not permitted, the work is done by influencing human beings, and that "men of good will" on earth can be used consciously or unconsciously to influence and support those who have the direct responsibility for taking decisions. I say "consciously or unconsciously" because all is done by the power of thought, and constructive, helpful thoughts are useful and used from whatever quarter they come.

Also remember that all cynical and defeatist thoughts about the United Nations or similar organisations are actively pernicious and harmful, so avoid such thoughts and check such conversation so far as you are able.

As has more than once been said to me, "The salvation of mankind must come through man." And so I say that these, our great guardians and friends, though they may never have been Christians on earth, are now Christians in the widest sense of the term in that they serve under the banner of the Christ Spirit. The word Christ is but a name (though it is indeed a name of power), and it is expressed by other words in other languages and creeds. It remains nevertheless the same—the unifying foundation of the common religion of heaven and earth. Or better, perhaps, the religion of heaven which will become the common religion of earth also when the Truth becomes known.

It seems to me an unprofitable exercise that man should strain his imagination here on earth in an attempt to visualise the nature of God. The conception is so far beyond the powers of our limited three-dimensional senses that the attempt can but end in frustration and futility.

According to my way of looking at things the combination of Jesus Christ, though perhaps far beyond our powers of full comprehension, is nevertheless a conception which we can reasonably hold in our imagination—a human being over shadowed and inspired by a direct emanation from the Divine.

And we can think of that combination as having a special relation to each one of us as a mediator or intermediary between ourselves and whatever lies beyond.

As I say, we shall do well to avoid crystallising our ideas too sharply on this subject. The greatest ones with whom we can make contact profess to know little more than we do. If logical thought is any guide, perhaps there is some pyramidical hierarchy stretching up through rulers of the earth, the Solar System, the Galaxies and Nebulae, the Universes to the Universal Intelligence.

On the other hand we are taught by our teachers that each one of us is a part of God, and that, being parts of God, we are also parts of one another. That the idea that we are not constitutes the Illusion of Separateness which must be overcome at some stage on our onward journey. The same teaching holds that the animals and the plants and even the so-called "inanimate" minerals are all parts of God—in fact that God is the Universe.

This is a hard teaching to accept while the Illusion of Separateness persists, and for the time being I don't think it is necessary to do more than to let it simmer in the back of our minds; but one thing is important—this universal and comprehensive way of regarding God never leads to His being considered as a sort of natural phenomenon, a sort of lake of spiritual power, in the eyes of those who are nearer to comprehension of Him than we are. His Name they do not speak. In worship and humility they refer to The Absolute, The Ultimate, The Nameless One. Let us not attempt to be wiser than they.

THE ETHERIC DOUBLE

Now I think that I must try to give an abbreviated account of some of the lower bodies of man and of his progress after physical death. I have given a fuller account in Chapters 4 and 12 of *Lychgate*, although that account itself is only a brief and somewhat dogmatic condensation of a very vast subject.

A good many people will accept the truism that man is a spirit here and now and that he assumes the physical body at birth like a cloak and lays it aside at physical death. This is true enough, but it is only a partial truth, because the essential spirit of man is clothed in a number of vestures of which the physical body is only the outermost and last.

Everything in nature (I believe) has what is called an etheric double. Man and animals and plants certainly have. This body is actually material, though invisible and impalpable. It is composed of a grade of physical matter finer than what we know as gaseous, and intermediate between that state and the ultimate physical atom.

This etheric double is intimately connected with the health of the body and with its processes of growth.

It is in fact the intermediary between the brain and nervous system, and the various currents of thought-matter and emotion-matter which affect them from the outside.

In a normal "natural death" the etheric double and higher bodies are slowly withdrawn from the physical (a process which can be actually seen by some clairvoyants), and then the etheric double is in turn discarded. But in cases of sudden or violent death it frequently happens that there is no time to discard the etheric double—the soul, in fact, has never for an instant lost consciousness—and this is the main reason accounting for the fact that those individuals, whose awakening I have described above, did not know that they were dead. Probably, if we could have followed their subsequent movements, we should learn that they were somewhere given the opportunity of having a good sleep, during which the disposal of the etheric double would have been arranged.

Here I will pause to interpolate a story which illustrates and confirms this idea of the etheric double, which you may be inclined to repudiate on account of its novelty. It is one of a dozen stories received by a friend of mine and published over my name in the *Sunday Pictorial* in June, 1943.

It relates to a pilot who was shot down in France. He was shot through the head and killed instantaneously.

"The next thing I knew," says the pilot, "was that I was standing beside the plane which was all crashed up, and my observer was lying beside me. I tried to help him and get him up, but I was too weak to move him.

"I thought it must be due to shock, and then, turning towards the plane, I saw another figure hunched over the controls. I rushed up to free him and found to my horror that it was myself—I had come apart from my body—that was what had happened. It was a most helpless feeling. I didn't at first connect it with being dead. I just felt horrified at finding my own wrecked body. I couldn't think what to do; there was Clarke lying unconscious, perhaps dead, and I was in this awful separated condition.

"I waited over him and got so tired that I lay down and seemed to unconsciously leave my second body—it was like shelling peas—there was one of me in the plane, another of me lying near, and still I seemed to go on and be just as much myself outside both of them." This is very unusual, remarkable and important. The pilot in his new personality, consisting of his astral and higher bodies, could see simultaneously his physical body and its etheric double. The observer, on the other hand, was still entangled with his etheric double.

The pilot continues: "As I came outside my second body I met Clarke. He was wandering about looking absolutely lost. He caught sight of the plane, but I managed to draw him away, not wanting him to see all our bodies lying about.

It really gives one an awful shock to see onself." Then a stranger came along to help them. The pilot could see and converse with him, but poor Clarke didn't seem to be able to see him and kept asking where they were.

After a time they came to a house and garden with seats in it and Clarke fell into one of the seats and went off to sleep at once.

"The stranger told me," said the pilot, "that we had come to the Garden of Awakening, but it wasn't necessary for me, as I had already left my second body behind. This was the place where the soul shakes off the last remnants of earth, but I had done that when I fell asleep outside the plane... Apparently the physical body has a sort of inner half which is partly physical and has to be got rid of before one can see and hear properly over here; and until that happens some fellows go through a difficult time—one doesn't really belong to any sphere. I was lucky." To return to my interrupted explanation, entanglement with the etheric double results in the earth-bound condition. A wandering in a sort of grey mist between the physical world and that world, next above it, in the cosmic scale, which is called the astral or the emotional sphere.

The word 'astral' of course, means starry' and is taken from the luminous quality of the astral body which becomes apparent as soon as that body is detached from its two lower bodies, the etheric and the physical.

The astral sphere, with its seven planes, covers a very wide range of conditions. To use Roman Catholic phrase-ology, it includes Paradise, Purgatory and Hell.

One of the things which you must look out for when studying this subject, is the different meaning which is attached to the same words by different authors. Some people, for instance, use the same word for what I have called etheric and astral.

One can accept any terminology without saying that it is either 'right' or 'wrong,' so long as an idea is retained of the difference between etheric and astral matter. The former though impalpable is physical, whereas the latter is not.

Another source of overlapping arises in the use of the words 'spirit' and 'soul' where in wide divergences of practice exist. I claim no special authority for my own use of the word soul as the spirit plus the lower bodies of the personality which it may be inhabiting at the time,' when a distinction is important; but on most occasions either word can be used indifferently without causing confusion.

It is rather pedantic and clumsy to insist on the use of the word 'soul' when speaking of 'evil spirits' or 'malicious spirits' or 'unprogressed spirits,' to which term the ear has become accustomed.

It is in the astral sphere then, that the soul finds itself on awakening instantaneously, or after a long or short delay, after physical death; and you may wonder what principle determines the 'place' to which the soul gravitates, between the extremes of the brightest paradise or the darkest hell.

The answer, I think, is to be found in the circumstance that the brightness of the different grades of the astral corresponds to a definite scale of wavelengths or vibrations, that the soul during earth-life has built for itself a definite vibrational wavelength, and that the soul cannot tolerate a surrounding condition of wavelengths finer or brighter than its own. (I say 'brighter' because, to a soul which attempts to wander above its own level, the inhibiting effect is one of glaring and intolerable brightness).

So it is indeed true that each one of us goes 'to his own place.' Life in the astral is ultimately devoted to the mastery of the emotional body, or the body of the desires. In the lower strata of the astral all the physical desires remain with out the physical means of gratifying them. Free will exists there, as here; and the interplay of these uncontrolled and unsatisfied desires constitutes hell.

We haven't been given nearly as much information about hell as about the other parts of the astral, and it would be a morbid and unhealthy curiosity which sought to probe too deeply into the details of the unhappy state of its inhabitants; but if you will picture to yourself a dark and gloomy world where might is right, where men are ruled by fear alone, where anger, hatred, envy, malice and all uncharitableness flourish unchecked, you will readily understand that man's inhumanity to man is all that is needed (except in the very lowest depths), to mete out the discipline necessary for eventual regeneration.

I want to stress that the most awful part of this experience is the sense of being "forgotten by God," of being completely and irrevocably at the mercy of cruel or evil men, hopelessly out of touch with any good influence or any house of rescue.

But this sense, although deliberately imposed for the sake of eventual progress, is quite fallacious. Every incident and every reaction of every soul is watched and meticulously recorded, so that, when the proper time comes, the rescuing messengers may be sent on their errand of mercy and may bring forth the soul which is ready for the experience into the lesser darkness and eventually into the greater light.

I speak with the humility of ignorance, but I do not think that a high proportion of the human race pass through these depths; only those, I think, who have deliberately and of fixed purpose set up their puny wills in opposition to the Source of all Power and Light.

Then there is a large section of the astral population which exists in a rather stagnant fashion in conditions approximating to those of earth. The inhabitants of these levels appear to wear earth-clothes, to continue their earth-occupations in a vague sort of way and apparently to consume earth food.

Letters from a Living Dead Man, by Elsa Barker gives a graphic account of those in this condition. I think that this, like so many of these books, is out of print now, but it is a well-known book and obtainable from most psychic libraries.

One can turn with relief from these levels to the higher strata of the astral—known to many as "The Summerland." This is where true progress is made. Here are the great colleges of Science and Music and Colour. Here the power of creative thought is harnessed and trained and exercised.

All is bright and smiling and carefree. Every innocuous desire can be gratified by the exercise of thought alone and yet this is not the true heaven, it is only paradise, there is still something lacking.

That something, for which the soul now begins to yearn, is emancipation from the lower emotions and desires. The sense of possessiveness ceases to satisfy when anything not actually harmful can be possessed merely by making the necessary mental effort.

The conditions of existence become too saccharine, the soul senses the danger of stagnation, and finally the time comes for the next step— out of the astral sphere altogether into the sphere next above, which is generally termed the Mental.

This transition is called by my teachers the "Second Death." It is not associated with any idea of fear or pain, but is a glad and happy ceremony of graduation, similar to the transition from school to a university.

At this stage the astral body is discarded, as were the physical body and etheric double at physical death, and resolved again into its constituent particles of astral matter.

The soul has now reached the Lower Heaven, and it proceeds on its path of continuous development, this time to develop and in due course to discard the mental body, which has now become the "outer skin of the onion", to adopt a useful simile.

Of course, one needn't wait until the second death to begin the development and discipline of the mental body.

We can and should begin now, and very difficult it is too.

An undisciplined mental body is responsible for all those futile trains of thought into which we allow our uncontrolled minds to wander.

I suppose an Anglican Church Service is one of the most fertile fields for this sort of activity, because through countless vain repetitions the words have become difficult to hold in sharp focus.

This sort of thing: Parson. Dearly beloved brethren . . .

Lower Mental. Brethren—Haven't seen my brother for a long time—Last I heard he was at Weston Super Mare—I never know how to pronounce that, "Mary" or "Mare"— I wonder what happened to that little mare Skittles I had in India—I won my first race on her—I remember how sick old Snooks was at being beaten—wonder what's happened to Snooks—didn't someone tell me that he'd been killed in Burma? —Gosh, what a show that jungle fighting must have been— imagine being the leading man having to force your way through the jungle never knowing when the balloon would go up—and the rains and the leeches—you must never pull a leech off because it leaves its teeth in you—I remember the leeches in Ceylon—wish I'd had the energy to go to those buried Cities when I was there—etc.—etc. And by the time your attention has returned the Te Deum is beginning, when off you go on another mental journey initiated by the sight of a bald head or some equally insignificant object.

All this is futile and fatuous but comparatively harmless.

The trouble is that the habit of mental indiscipline permits the mind to cooperate with the emotions in some very undesirable activities on occasions. Suppose for instance that you hear that someone has done you an injury—repeated some slanderous story to your employer, for instance. Perhaps a great flash of scarlet anger goes out from your emotional body. That's bad enough, but if it is allowed to die out at once perhaps there's not much harm done. But now suppose you let your mind reinforce your emotions and build up strong thought-forms of hate, and indulge yourself in spinning complicated schemes of revenge, you are pushing out a great deal of stuff which may or may not injure the object of your hatred, but which is most certainly going to hurt you a great deal more when it returns, as it will, to roost.

So it is most important to practise mind-control here and now, and not allow yourself to be dragged hither and yon in the trail of an undisciplined imagination. I think that most of this work will be completed before the second death, and that the subsequent training will be more in the nature of educating and expanding the intuition than in disciplining the lower mind.

The importance of the intuition is constantly impressed on us. As I understand it, it consists of a sort of coupling-up of the mind to the Universal Intelligence, so that we may reach the shores of knowledge which lie deeply hidden in the sub-consciousness of every human being, so that true inspiration may be always available at need, so that we may no longer have to depend on the restricted operation of the lower mind.

There have been men, and there are now men living on earth who can attain to this coupling-up process during their physical lives and can tap the source of true inspiration.

Of such are the great prophets of the past and the great though generally unknown seers of the present day. I am not now speaking of mediums. In one sense all seers are mediums, but very few mediums are seers.

The distinction depends upon the level at which contact with the unseen can be made.

And this is where I propose to leave you to continue your own studies and to find your own way, if you are interested. Theosophy and

Buddhism may help you along the road to knowledge and wisdom, but don't become a slavish follower of any person's ideas whether that person is in or out of the physical body. The discarnate can be just as wrong as we can, and their errors are the more serious since they have the spurious authority which is instinctively attributed by us to people in their position.

As a mental cud on which to chew I will leave you with the thought: Does it seem reasonable to you that a spirit, which has as its destiny a descent into earth incarnation, should rely on one single turn of the wheel to acquire all the experience which it requires for its eternal progress? If so, how can you account in justice for a life spent as an idiot, or for a life terminated at birth? To quote Sir Edwin Arnold's translation of the Bhagavad-Gita:

Never the spirit was born; the spirit shall cease to be never; never was time it was not; End and beginning are dreams.
Birthless and deathless and changeless remaineth the spirit forever.
Death hath not touched it at all, dead though the house of it seems.

The human mind commonly has an instinctive revulsion from the idea of returning again to a milieu where, upon the whole, sorrow and pain and frustration and apprehension have outweighed the pleasures and amenities of life. But after all it is illogical to refuse to believe anything merely on the grounds that it is distasteful to us. Many well-meaning and earnest persons believe in the actuality of eternal punishment in hell, and if they can swallow that camel they should not strain at the gnat of rebirth.

Perhaps you are not interested in these speculations, or have no leisure or opportunity to study. If so it doesn't very much matter. The task which I have set myself in this little book is to try to draw you past the first stepping stone of Spiritualism—the proof of survival and the possibility of communication—past this on to an intelligent speculation into the conditions of life after death, and an acceptance of the idea that the True Self is something very much greater than the Personality which the Self builds up for a single lifetime, limiting itself by the addition of the four transient bodies (Mental, Astral, Etheric and Physical), to which I have referred above.

If you can accept this idea, then you will be ready to consider at least the advisability of leading a life, on earth and in the after stages, which shall be to the benefit of that True Self and not of the transient Personality.

You will also be open to consider the idea that eternity is here and now, that life is continuous in and through all spheres, and that what you do in this world is important because you are actually creating the conditions in which you will pass the first stages of your continuing life after death. There is a story of a rich and selfish man who complained bitterly to the Messenger who showed him the mean hovel which was to be his new home in the astral. "These are all the materials which you have sent over," was the reply.

The word 'Religion' has many definitions, but my definition of it is "action in accordance with enlightened Self interest," instead of "unenlightened self-interest." I believe that much that was and is taught under the name of the 'Ancient Wisdom' is true, has been true since ages before the birth of Jesus, and will be true for untold ages to come. But with this Ancient Wisdom must be blended the message of The Christ, as given by those who have been overshadowed by His Spirit, and, in its complete form, through our Beloved Master Jesus—the message of self-sacrifice and love.

That is one thing. And the other thing I should like you to do is to look on Spiritualism not merely as something from which its devotees can obtain gratifications by the witnessing of signs and wonders and the assuagement of their grief through contacts with those whom they love, but as a means of making a personal contribution to the needs of humanity on both sides of the grave, working with those unseen ones with whom our lives are intertwined.

And you can take part in this work, though you may never go to a Spiritualist service nor attend a séance. You can do it by the power of thought, now especially, when so many of the world's problems are in the melting pot. You can send out strong constructive thoughts of unity and brotherhood to the Council of the United Nations, when they are in session, to the meetings of the representatives of the great powers when they are trying to reach agreement on peace treaties, to the councils of those who are striving to settle the Indian or the Palestinian questions, and you are never likely to know in this world how much you have helped! Here I stop, and I will let Chang say goodnight to you for me:

And now, as the voices of the rivers sing Thy praise, as the dancing leaves cry Glory, Glory unto Thee, as the flowers perfume the air in the evening, as the rocks give forth heat in joy, as the winds waft the voices of the children of men in praise—so do we join Thy great symphony, and offer thanks for all that we have received and all that we are to receive.

As incense rises into the still air, so rise our thoughts to The Great One, whose Name we dare not utter for the love which floods our beings. Let us rest with Thee.

FURTHER READING

What Spiritualism is by Horace Leaf

The Healing Pathway by "White Wing" through Rebecca Williams

The Evolutions of Religion as portrayed by a Spiritualist by Robert T. Rossiter

The Effect of Religion on History by J. Arthur Findlay, M.B.E.

A Guide for the Development of Mediumship by Harry Edwards

The Mystery of the Human Aura by Ursula Roberts

Journey into Spirit World by Bertha Harris

Attention All Spiritualists by Bennu, through the hand of Reg Burwell

Paperbacks also available from
White Crow Books

Elsa Barker—*Letters from
a Living Dead Man*
ISBN 978-1-907355-83-7

Elsa Barker—*War Letters from
the Living Dead Man*
ISBN 978-1-907355-85-1

Elsa Barker—*Last Letters from
the Living Dead Man*
ISBN 978-1-907355-87-5

Richard Maurice Bucke—
Cosmic Consciousness
ISBN 978-1-907355-10-3

Arthur Conan Doyle—
The Edge of the Unknown
ISBN 978-1-907355-14-1

Arthur Conan Doyle—
The New Revelation
ISBN 978-1-907355-12-7

Arthur Conan Doyle—
The Vital Message
ISBN 978-1-907355-13-4

Arthur Conan Doyle with
Simon Parke—*Conversations
with Arthur Conan Doyle*
ISBN 978-1-907355-80-6

Meister Eckhart with Simon Parke—
Conversations with Meister Eckhart
ISBN 978-1-907355-18-9

D. D. Home—*Incidents in my Life Part 1*
ISBN 978-1-907355-15-8

Mme. Dunglas Home; edited,
with an Introduction, by Sir
Arthur Conan Doyle—*D. D.
Home: His Life and Mission*
ISBN 978-1-907355-16-5

Edward C. Randall—
Frontiers of the Afterlife
ISBN 978-1-907355-30-1

Rebecca Ruter Springer—
Intra Muros: My Dream of Heaven
ISBN 978-1-907355-11-0

Leo Tolstoy, edited by Simon
Parke—*Forbidden Words*
ISBN 978-1-907355-00-4

Leo Tolstoy—*A Confession*
ISBN 978-1-907355-24-0

Leo Tolstoy—*The Gospel in Brief*
ISBN 978-1-907355-22-6

Leo Tolstoy—*The Kingdom
of God is Within You*
ISBN 978-1-907355-27-1

Leo Tolstoy—*My Religion:
What I Believe*
ISBN 978-1-907355-23-3

Leo Tolstoy—*On Life*
ISBN 978-1-907355-91-2

Leo Tolstoy—*Twenty-three Tales*
ISBN 978-1-907355-29-5

Leo Tolstoy—*What is Religion
and other writings*
ISBN 978-1-907355-28-8

Leo Tolstoy—*Work While
Ye Have the Light*
ISBN 978-1-907355-26-4

Leo Tolstoy—*The Death of Ivan Ilyich*
ISBN 978-1-907661-10-5

Leo Tolstoy—*Resurrection*
ISBN 978-1-907661-09-9

Leo Tolstoy with Simon Parke—
Conversations with Tolstoy
ISBN 978-1-907355-25-7

Howard Williams with an Introduction
by Leo Tolstoy—*The Ethics of Diet:
An Anthology of Vegetarian Thought*
ISBN 978-1-907355-21-9

Vincent Van Gogh with Simon Parke—
Conversations with Van Gogh
ISBN 978-1-907355-95-0

Wolfgang Amadeus Mozart with Simon
Parke—*Conversations with Mozart*
ISBN 978-1-907661-38-9

Jesus of Nazareth with Simon Parke—
Conversations with Jesus of Nazareth
ISBN 978-1-907661-41-9

Thomas à Kempis with Simon
Parke—*The Imitation of Christ*
ISBN 978-1-907661-58-7

Julian of Norwich with Simon
Parke—*Revelations of Divine Love*
ISBN 978-1-907661-88-4

Allan Kardec—*The Spirits Book*
ISBN 978-1-907355-98-1

Allan Kardec—*The Book on Mediums*
ISBN 978-1-907661-75-4

Emanuel Swedenborg—*Heaven and Hell*
ISBN 978-1-907661-55-6

P.D. Ouspensky—*Tertium Organum:
The Third Canon of Thought*
ISBN 978-1-907661-47-1

Dwight Goddard—*A Buddhist Bible*
ISBN 978-1-907661-44-0

Michael Tymn—*The Afterlife Revealed*
ISBN 978-1-970661-90-7

Michael Tymn—*Transcending the
Titanic: Beyond Death's Door*
ISBN 978-1-908733-02-3

Guy L. Playfair—*If This Be Magic*
ISBN 978-1-907661-84-6

Guy L. Playfair—*The Flying Cow*
ISBN 978-1-907661-94-5

Guy L. Playfair —*This House is Haunted*
ISBN 978-1-907661-78-5

Carl Wickland, M.D.—
Thirty Years Among the Dead
ISBN 978-1-907661-72-3

John E. Mack—*Passport to the Cosmos*
ISBN 978-1-907661-81-5

Peter & Elizabeth Fenwick—
The Truth in the Light
ISBN 978-1-908733-08-5

Erlendur Haraldsson—
Modern Miracles
ISBN 978-1-908733-25-2

Erlendur Haraldsson—
At the Hour of Death
ISBN 978-1-908733-27-6

Erlendur Haraldsson—
The Departed Among the Living
ISBN 978-1-908733-29-0

Brian Inglis—*Science and Parascience*
ISBN 978-1-908733-18-4

Brian Inglis—*Natural and Supernatural:
A History of the Paranormal*
ISBN 978-1-908733-20-7

Ernest Holmes—*The Science of Mind*
ISBN 978-1-908733-10-8

Victor & Wendy Zammit —*A Lawyer
Presents the Evidence For the Afterlife*
ISBN 978-1-908733-22-1

Casper S. Yost—*Patience
Worth: A Psychic Mystery*
ISBN 978-1-908733-06-1

William Usborne Moore—
Glimpses of the Next State
ISBN 978-1-907661-01-3

William Usborne Moore—
The Voices
ISBN 978-1-908733-04-7

John W. White—
The Highest State of Consciousness
ISBN 978-1-908733-31-3

Stafford Betty—
The Imprisoned Splendor
ISBN 978-1-907661-98-3

Paul Pearsall, Ph.D. —
Super Joy
ISBN 978-1-908733-16-0

**All titles available as eBooks, and selected titles available in Hardback and
Audiobook formats from www.whitecrowbooks.com**

Lightning Source UK Ltd.
Milton Keynes UK
UKOW02f0348191116
288027UK00005B/350/P